Contents

SIMPLE MEDITERRANEAN COOKERY

CLAUDIA RODEN

SIMPLE MEDITERRANEAN COOKERY

CLAUDIA
RODEN

Step by step to
everyone's favourite
Mediterranean recipes

BBC
BOOKS

About the author

Claudia Roden was born and brought up in Cairo. She finished her education in Paris and then moved to London to study art. Since her childhood she has travelled extensively throughout the Mediterranean and has won five Glenfiddich Awards, including 'Food Writer of the Year' in 1992. Her other books include *A New Book of Middle Eastern Food*, *Coffee*, *Picnic*, *Sainsbury's Middle Eastern Cooking*, *Mediterranean Cookery*, and the award-winning *The Book of Jewish Food*.

Dedication
For my children, Simon, Nadia and Anna, and their families.

Food photography by Jean Cazals

Published by BBC Books,
BBC Worldwide Ltd,
Woodlands,
80 Wood Lane,
London W12 0TT

First published in hardback as *Foolproof Mediterranean Cookery* in 2003
This paperback edition first published in 2006
Copyright © Claudia Roden 2003
The moral right of Claudia Roden to be identified as the author of this work has been asserted.

Food photography © Jean Cazals 2003

ISBN 0 563 49327 5

Commissioning editors: Nicky Ross and Rachel Copus
Project editor: Sarah Lavelle
Copy editor: Jane Middleton
Art direction and design: Lisa Pettibone
Home economist: Marie Ange Lapierre
Stylist: Sue Rowlands

The publishers would like to thank the following for supplying items used in the photographs: David Mellor, Divertimenti, Kara Kara and Sumerill and Bishop.

Set in Univers
Printed and bound in Italy by Printer Trento Srl
Colour separations by Kestrel Digital Colour, Chelmsford

Introduction

Mediterranean food is famously popular all over the world. The Mediterranean diet – rich in grains, vegetables, pulses, fruit and nuts, with little meat, plenty of fish, and olive oil as the main fat – has long been adopted as a model of healthy eating.

But its real appeal is the sensual quality of the cooking, which is full of rich flavours, aromas and colours, as well as its simplicity. It is the kind of food I love. I am sure you will want to adopt it for your everyday cooking, as well as for entertaining.

I have been travelling around the Mediterranean researching the cooking for decades now. I was born in Egypt and, as they say, if you belong to any part of the Mediterranean you are never a stranger along its shores. I feel at home with the architecture and the street life, the way people live, the way they shop and cook and eat. There is great regional diversity between the 16 or so countries around the Mediterranean, yet there are also many similarities. I found the same ingredients and many similar dishes from one end of the sea to the other. It has to do with the shared climate and produce, the age-old trading between the port cities, and an incestuous history, with the same empires and influences – Roman, Greek, Arab, Ottoman, Spanish – spreading across the region.

The recipes I picked for this book are some of the favourites I enjoyed on my travels and which I like to make at home. Dishes such as these, which have a history and are part of an old culture and tradition, have a special charm. You will love them too.

Ingredients and Equipment

INGREDIENTS

All ingredients used in Mediterranean cooking are generally available in the UK. Below is some useful information on the ingredients featured in this book.

Aubergines

The aubergine is the favourite vegetable of the Mediterranean. Choose firm, medium-sized ones with shiny, unblemished skin. If you are not going to fry them, you do not need to salt them to remove their bitter juices. The aubergines produced these days are only pleasantly bitter. Salting them does, however, mean that they absorb a little less oil, which is an advantage as they normally soak up so much. Grilling and roasting aubergines is a good way of avoiding that.

Bread

In the Mediterranean bread is present at every meal. It is used to pick up morsels of food, to dip into a creamy salad and to soak up sauces. It goes at the bottom of a juicy salad and in a bowl of soup; it is pounded into a sauce with olive oil; and crumbs are sprinkled over a gratin. The simplest appetizer in the western Mediterranean is a slice of bread smeared with olive oil and rubbed with garlic or tomatoes, or spread with an olive and anchovy paste.

The variety of breads that you find in the area, from the very thin, floppy breads baked on a griddle in the eastern Mediterranean to the great, round loaves of southern Italy, is extraordinary. The ever-increasing range available here is already substantial. Apart from the flat, pouched pitta, Italian ciabatta and focaccia, Spanish *pan gallego* and French baguette and country breads you can find in supermarkets, ethnic shops (mainly Turkish, Lebanese and Cypriot) and specialist bakeries now sell a wide variety of Mediterranean breads. There are different kinds of Lebanese flat breads, some exquisitely thin and light, some sprinkled with wild thyme, sesame seeds and sumac or flavoured with onions or garlic and herbs; Turkish sesame rings and huge, thick, soft, flat breads like focaccia; Greek olive breads and sesame loaves; Spanish *pan de borona* made with maize flour; Italian herb and olive oil and walnut and raisin breads.

Bulgur

Bulgur, a staple of Turkey and the Arab world, is wheat that has been boiled and dried, then ground to various degrees of fineness. The

Above: aubergines

Above: a selection of Mediterranean breads

Above: couscous (left), bulgur (right) and filo pastry underneath.

one available in supermarkets is medium-ground. It is used in salads and as a pilaf and is very easy to prepare, as it only needs to soak up water or stock and requires little or no cooking.

Capers

Capers are the pickled buds of a bush that grows wild in the Mediterranean. The best capers are preserved in salt rather than in brine or vinegar. Sometimes they are pickled on the branch, complete with thorns and leaves. They are good in salads and as a garnish for fish.

Cheeses

Mediterranean cheeses are made mostly from sheep's or goat's milk. They can be eaten for breakfast with olives, or as an appetizer – grilled, fried or simply cut into pieces. Feta and halloumi are the cheeses of the Middle East; pecorino, mozzarella and ricotta are used in southern Italy. The South of France produces a large selection of cheese for eating and uses Gruyère and Parmesan in cooking. Spanish cheeses include manchego, a firm sheep's milk cheese; the square, semi-soft mahon, made from cow's milk; and majorero, made from goat's milk.

The flavour of freshly grated Parmesan is far superior to that of the packaged, ready-grated type, so buy a piece and grate it as you need it – make sure you always buy Parmigiano Reggiano. It keeps in the refrigerator if you wrap it up well. Aged pecorino can be grated like Parmesan but it is very much sharper and is best used only in dishes featuring strong flavours.

Couscous

Couscous, a North African staple, is hard wheat that has been ground to various degrees of fineness, then moistened and coated with fine flour. It is traditionally cooked by lengthy steaming. The mass-produced varieties available in the UK are pre-cooked. They really only need to have water added (the same volume as its own) and to be heated through, but you can then make it light and fluffy by rubbing it between your hands.

Dried fruit

Sun-dried prunes, apricots, figs, raisins and currants are used in savoury dishes with meat and chicken as well as in sweet ones.

Filo pastry

A speciality of the eastern Mediterranean, this paper-thin pastry is now common all over the world. You can buy it fresh or frozen in super-markets and some delicatessens. The sheets come in different sizes and different degrees of thinness.

Packs should not remain in the freezer for longer than three months, otherwise ice crystals form and, when these melt, the sheets stick together and tear when you try to separate them. Frozen filo must be allowed to defrost slowly for 2–3 hours. Open the packet just before you need it and then use the sheets as

Clockwise from bottom left: halloumi, Gruyère, Parmesan, mozzarella and feta

quickly as possible, otherwise they will become dry and brittle in the air. Keep the sheets in a pile so that the air does not dry them out. If you have to leave them for a few minutes, cover with a slightly damp cloth or cling film.

Fish

Nearly all Mediterranean fish are now available in the UK – sea bass, bream, tuna, hake, red mullet, monkfish, John Dory, grouper, sardines, skate, turbot and swordfish. You can substitute other kinds of fish in most recipes, if necessary.

Do get into the habit of cooking fish. The more familiar you are with it, the more you will enjoy it. Try to buy fish and seafood the day you want to eat it because it spoils very quickly. When you buy fish it must be absolutely fresh and smell of the sea. The eyes must be bright and clear, the gills bright pink or red and the flesh firm. When you press it with your finger it should not leave an indentation, and when you pick it up it should not flop. Shellfish and, if possible, crustaceans should be bought alive. Ask the fishmonger to scale, clean, fillet or skin fish; he or she should be happy to prepare it any way you want it.

Canned tuna preserved in brine or spring water is better, to my taste, than that preserved in oil because the oil used is not the best. Anchovy fillets are sold preserved in oil or in salt. The latter should be soaked in water to remove excess salt.

Garlic

Garlic is said to be the truffle of the Mediterranean and is believed to have health-giving properties. Its aroma is all-pervading. There are different kinds – white, mauve and pink-skinned, planted in the spring and autumn. Young garlic has a fresh taste and juicy flesh, while garlic that can be aged for up to 14 months is considered a *grand cru* in Provence.

Choose heads of garlic that are firm (they should not be sprouting) and keep them in a dry place.

Herbs

Basil, marjoram, thyme, rosemary, sage, chervil and chives are common in the western and northern Mediterranean, mint and coriander in the east and south. Flat-leaf parsley is ubiquitous. Keep your herbs in a glass of water or in a bag (paper or plastic) in the refrigerator.

Basil
Basil characterizes the flavour of southern French and Italian cooking. There is a very large-leafed variety (as large as spinach) and a smaller-leafed type that has a stronger flavour. Dried basil is no substitute for fresh.

Bay
Bay leaves are used fresh or dried. They are cooked with meat and fish (threaded on skewers for kebabs) and also lend their flavour to sauces, soups and stews.

Coriander
Mountains of fresh coriander are a common sight in Middle Eastern markets. The leaves are chopped up into salads and give a special flavour to soups, sauces and stews.

Clockwise from bottom left: anchovy fillets, tuna steak and whole red mullet

Clockwise from top: basil, coriander, marjoram, rosemary, mint and dill (centre)

Dill

The feathery, slightly aniseedy leaves of dill are commonly used in Greece and Turkey.

Marjoram

There are many different species of this herb growing wild. It goes particularly well with tomatoes and is commonly sprinkled on pizzas.

Mint

Spearmint is much loved and used extensively in the Mediterranean, both fresh and dried. People dry it themselves and crush it over a dish by rubbing a few leaves between their hands. It is popular in salads and goes well with yoghurt and cheese. It also gives a refreshing flavour to cooked vegetables that are to be eaten cold. In Morocco mint tea is the most popular drink.

Parsley

It is preferable to use flat-leaf parsley, which has a stronger flavour than the usual curly British kind. Use it very generously.

Rosemary

This Italian herb is used especially when roasting or grilling chicken and lamb. It is better fresh, so try growing it in your garden – it always does well.

Thyme

Wild thyme grows mostly in France and Greece. A cultivated variety is easy to grow at home.

Honey

The fragrance of honey depends on the flowers on which the bees have fed. Greeks use honey in their sweets and pastries. In Morocco it is also added to savoury dishes, with delicious results. As it is only used in small quantities it is always worth buying a really good honey. The best is made from the nectar of thyme and rosemary flowers, and spring honey is better than autumn. Honeys from Hymethus in Greece and from Narbonne, Gatenais and Champagne in France are highly esteemed.

Lemons

Lemon juice is used to flavour and season a great number of dishes, and you can detect its presence in stews and sauces. Lemon wedges are often served to squeeze over appetizers, where the sharp flavour has the effect of whetting the appetite, and over grilled meat or fish. Thin-skinned lemons have more juice. See also Pickled or preserved lemons on page 17.

Nuts

Almonds, pistachios and pine nuts are the most common nuts in Mediterranean countries. They are used frequently as garnishes, to thicken soups, stews and sauces, and in savoury dishes, as well as in pastries and puddings. They are sometimes toasted for a moment before use to bring out their flavour.

Olive oil

Olive oil is an important traditional agricultural product of the Mediterranean. An extraordinarily wide range of olive oils is now available in the UK, varying in taste, colour and aroma. The extra-virgin oils produced from first cold pressings are the finest, and the richest in flavour and scent. Oils can be light and delicate or assertive and strong; their flavours sweet, fruity, nutty, spicy, peppery or bitter, and their fragrances floral, fruity, nutty, grassy, elusive or intense.

Although you cannot really generalize, the oils of Provence tend to be light, sweet and fragrant, the oils of Greece hearty, slightly bitter and assertive, while Portuguese oils are rough and rustic. Spanish oils vary from the aromatic, almondy Catalans to the sweet, fruity Andalusians. Tuscany is famous for the strong, bitter flavour and peppery aftertaste of its oils, and Puglia for its rich, fruity, peppery ones; while oils from Liguria, Umbria and the Abruzzi are light, sweet and fruity. Tunisian and Turkish oils are equally varied but not easily available in the UK.

The best extra-virgin oils should be used raw, as a dressing. I like a light, fresh, non-astringent, fragrant oil for salads, fish and boiled vegetables and to blend into delicate, uncooked sauces; and a rich, fruity oil for gazpachos and herby green sauces, to dress pasta and to drizzle over grilled or fried vegetables, meat or fish. A drop of strong-tasting, bitter, fruity or spicy oil will enhance the taste

Clockwise from bottom left: whole blanched almonds, pine nuts, clear honey and pistachio nuts

Clockwise from left: pickled/preserved lemons, green olives and kalamata olives

of a creamy soup, a stew or a tomato sauce and makes a rich dressing for pasta. For sauces that use plenty of oil, like mayonnaise, I mix a light vegetable oil such as sunflower with olive oil.

For deep-frying, use oils labelled refined olive oil or simply olive oil. These are produced from second or subsequent pressings, which have then been processed and refined and are usually quite bland. You can re-use olive oil after frying, but purify it by frying a lettuce leaf in it, then filter it to remove any bits before storing it in an airtight jar. Store olive oil in a cool place away from the light.

Olives

Olives are a symbol of the Mediterranean, and the limit of the olive tree defines the Mediterranean zone. They all ripen from green and yellow, through red and violet, to purple and black. Cured and preserved black and green olives are served for breakfast, as appetizers, and to accompany bread and cheese. They are also used in many different dishes. The main thing when buying olives is to pick a good-tasting variety. For this, you must sample them. Every Mediterranean country produces some very good ones. The fleshy Greek kalamata, the Spanish manzanilla and the large green Cerignola of Puglia, in Italy, are famous, as are the sweet, black, wrinkled olives of Provence and the tiny ones of Nice. Lately some very tasty Moroccan olives have come on the market.

Onions

The Mediterranean has many varieties of onion, including the fresh, white-bulbed ones, the smaller, more powerful ones, large Spanish and mild red Italian ones, shallots and spring onions. Many Mediterranean sauces and stews start with a base of chopped sautéed onions. They can also be braised, roasted, grilled or stuffed.

Orange-blossom water

The distilled essence of orange blossom adds a delicate perfume to many Mediterranean dishes and especially to the desserts of the eastern countries. In Morocco it is sometimes sprinkled over salads and also into stews. Use only a little, as it can be overpowering.

Pasta

Pasta is the everyday food of Italy, where there are reputedly 200 different kinds and shapes. Each type is said to make a difference to the taste as well as to the texture and appearance of the dish, because of the amount of sauce it is capable of collecting. It is best to buy dried pasta made with durum wheat, which preserves the wheatgerm, because this is the tastiest as well as the healthiest type. Its size trebles with cooking, it cooks evenly and does not get sticky.

Every country of the eastern Mediterranean also has some kind of pasta, in particular *rishta* (noodles), *lissan al assfour* (birds' tongues), which are added to meat stews, and *itriya* and *shaghria* (spaghetti and vermicelli), which are cooked with rice or served with a yoghurt topping, or cooked in milk with sugar for a pudding. Turkish *manti*, a stuffed pasta, is like the Chinese wonton and is Mongolian in origin.

Peppers

Like aubergines, peppers are one of the great vegetables of the Mediterranean. Red and yellow peppers are more mature than green ones, and the red ones are the sweetest. When they are roasted they acquire a lovely texture and delicious flavour. Choose firm, fleshy peppers.

Pickled or preserved lemons

You can now find lemons preserved in brine in some supermarkets. They give a distinctive flavour to Moroccan and North African *tagines* (stews) and salads. One variety of small, thin-skinned preserved lemon called *beldi* is particularly good. Normally the peel alone is used but some people like to throw in the pulp as well, especially with the very small ones.

Pulses

Pulses such as chickpeas, broad beans, lentils, haricot beans, black-eyed beans, borlotti and cannellini beans, and yellow and green split

Clockwise from top left: green lentils, chickpeas and red lentils

peas are used in soups, stews and salads, sometimes mashed to a purée. In this book I use split red lentils, which disintegrate with cooking, for a soup (see page 30) and large green or brown lentils combined with rice (see page 46). The advantage of lentils is that they do not need soaking in the way other pulses do.

Rice
Various kinds of rice are used around the Mediterranean, from long grain and basmati to short grain and round risotto rice. My favourite for making pilafs is basmati, because the grains remain separate and fluffy. Round rice (also called pudding rice) and risotto rice are used for puddings or stuffings because the grains stick together. Basmati rice has a delicate aroma. It needs washing before use.

Sesame seeds
Sesame seeds should be toasted lightly in a dry frying pan before use to bring out their full flavour.

Spices
Every country has its favourites. In Spain, the South of France and Morocco it is saffron, in Turkey it is cinnamon and allspice, while in Egypt it is cumin and coriander. Cumin is pervasive in North African fish dishes and appetizers.

Allspice
These dark brown berries resembling pepper-corns are ground and used in Arab and Turkish cooking to flavour meat, often together with cinnamon.

Caraway
Caraway seeds are used only in Tunisia and Turkey.

Cardamom
Brown, green or white cardamom pods are much used in the Arab world. They need to be cracked open to release their full flavour. You can also buy ready-ground cardamom.

Chilli
Chillies are used sparingly except in Tunisia and Algeria. Sometimes they are put whole into a dish to give it a kick and then removed before serving. Otherwise they are chopped up. They do not lose their pungency when dried.

Cinnamon
Cinnamon is used most extensively in the eastern Mediterranean. Spice merchants sell the dry brown bark more often in powder form. It gives a delicate perfume to minced meat fillings and to all kinds of meat and chicken stews. It is sprinkled over milk pud-dings and mixed with nuts in pastries.

Coriander
Coriander seeds are a very popular flavouring in the Arab part of the Mediterranean, where they are often teamed with cumin. You can buy them ready ground or you can grind them yourself. Crushed coriander frying in olive oil with garlic is a characteristic smell of Egypt.

Cumin
The thin, spindle-shaped, yellowish-brown seeds are responsible for one of the character-istic flavours of the Arab world. In Morocco

Clockwise from bottom left: cumin seeds, cinnamon sticks, cardamom pods and seeds, chilli powder, ginger and saffron threads (centre)

ground cumin is all pervading, especially in appetizers, since it is supposed to act as a digestive, and also in fish dishes. It is a component of the spice mixture *zahtar*, into which you dip bread soaked in oil.

Ginger
North Africa is the only part of the Mediterranean to use ground dried ginger, often in combination with cinnamon. In the western Mediterranean they use the fresh root.

Saffron
Saffron is the thread-like stamen of a violet-coloured crocus. It gives food a faint odour, an unusual, delicate, slightly bitter flavour and an intense yellow colour. The way to extract the best from the stamens is to crush them with the back of a teaspoon in a small cup or saucer before use.

Tomatoes
Tomatoes are ubiquitous in Mediterranean cooking – almost its signature flavour. The taste of the tomatoes we get at our green-grocer's and supermarkets has greatly improved in the last few years but it is still nothing like the intense flavour of the brilliant red plum tomatoes and the huge curvy, indented ones that have ripened in the Mediterranean sun. As the quality varies from shop to shop, it is difficult to name a type of tomato as the best to choose. At my local supermarket the plum tomatoes are the tastiest and that is what I generally use for sauces. Because of their shape, they will not do for all recipes – for example, stuffed tomatoes.

To skin tomatoes
Pour boiling water over the tomatoes and prick their skin with the point of a knife. Within a minute or so you will see the skin detaching itself from the flesh. Drain and pull off the skin.

Vinegar
Various vinegars are used in the Mediterranean, from sherry vinegar in Spain and cider vinegar in France to red and white wine vinegars. In recent times the sweet and sour balsamic vinegar, which was once only a speciality of Modena in Italy, has become fashionable. In the eastern Mediterranean the usual salad dressing is a mix of olive oil and lemon juice rather than vinegar.

Yoghurt
Yoghurt plays an important part in Ottoman and Arab cooking and accompanies many dishes. Buy natural, live, full-fat yoghurt or Greek-style strained yoghurt, which is thicker.

Above: large tomato, partially skinned (left), and plum tomato (right)

EQUIPMENT

All you really need to cook Mediterranean food is good knives, a wooden spoon, a mixing bowl, a wooden chopping board, a large frying pan, a saucepan and a baking dish. But you might also like to have traditional utensils, such as *tians* and *tagines*, for the pleasure and charm of using them.

Earthenware baking dish or pot
Every Mediterranean country has its own particular shape of glazed or unglazed earthenware dishes for baking. There are many beautiful ones around that you can buy. They are ovenproof and some can also go on the hob over a low heat. They hold the heat well and can be taken directly to the table to serve from. Mostly brown, they have a lovely rustic feel. A Spanish *olla* or *cazuela de barra* is round, usually with a curved bottom. A Provençal *tian* is oval. An Egyptian *tagen* has

straight sides, while a Moroccan *tagine* is round and shallow with a conical lid, like a pointed hat. A French *marmite* is a tall, straight-sided pot with a lid.

Food processor
I find mine invaluable for chopping, mashing and puréeing.

Frying pans
My favourites are a copper frying pan lined with stainless steel, which spreads the heat well, and a large non-stick one.

Garlic press
I use a metal one that I bought when I was a schoolgirl in Paris. A few that I have used in other people's homes have been no good at all, so I realized that it was important to have a sturdy one. I also use mine to extract the juice from fresh ginger root.

Grater
Choose one that can grate to different degrees of fineness. I use mine mainly to grate cheese and to extract orange and lemon zest.

Mezzaluna
This is a sickle-shaped, double-handled chopper, good for chopping herbs.

Pestle and mortar
You can choose from stone, marble and earthenware (I am not keen on metal ones). Use it to crush nuts, peppercorns or spices, or to mash garlic to a paste with a little salt.

Saucepans
If you like entertaining, it is good to own a large saucepan as well as a medium one. Heavy-based stainless steel pans give an all-round gentle heat. Although they use tinned

Clockwise from top left: grater, saucepan, copper frying pan, sieve and *tian*

copper pans in Mediterranean countries, and I have used them in the past, I do not recommend them because they need to be re-tinned at intervals.

Scales

More than three decades ago, when I started researching recipes among people from the eastern Mediterranean, no one ever had scales. They would say 'a handful' of this or of

that, and when dealing with dough they would say 'as much water as it takes'. Now we are used to scales, and they are invaluable when you start learning to cook.

Sieve or colander

You need a large sieve or colander with small holes for draining rice. I also use it when mashing the flesh of roasted aubergines, in order to let the juices run out.

Conversion tables

Conversions are approximate and have been rounded up or down. Follow one set of measurements only – do not mix metric and Imperial.

Weights		Volume		Measurements	
Metric	**Imperial**	**Metric**	**Imperial**	**Metric**	**Imperial**
15 g	½ oz	25 ml	1 fl oz	0.5 cm	¼ inch
25 g	1 oz	50 ml	2 fl oz	1 cm	½ inch
40 g	1½ oz	85 ml	3 fl oz	2.5 cm	1 inch
50 g	2 oz	150 ml	5 fl oz (¼ pint)	5 cm	2 inches
75 g	3 oz	300 ml	10 fl oz (½ pint)	7.5 cm	3 inches
100 g	4 oz	450 ml	15 fl oz (¾ pint)	10 cm	4 inches
150 g	5 oz	600 ml	1 pint	15 cm	6 inches
175 g	6 oz	700 ml	1¼ pints	18 cm	7 inches
200 g	7 oz	900 ml	1½ pints	20 cm	8 inches
225 g	8 oz	1 litres	1¾ pints	23 cm	9 inches
250 g	9 oz	1.2 litres	2 pints	25 cm	10 inches
275 g	10 oz	1.25 litres	2¼ pints	30 cm	12 inches
350 g	12 oz	1.5 litres	2½ pints		
375 g	13 oz	1.6 litres	2¾ pints		

Oven temperatures		
140°C	275°F	Gas Mk 1
150°C	300°F	Gas Mk 2
160°C	325°F	Gas Mk 3
180°C	350°F	Gas Mk 4
190°C	375°F	Gas Mk 5
200°C	400°F	Gas Mk 6
220°C	425°F	Gas Mk 7
230°C	450°F	Gas Mk 8
240°C	475°F	Gas Mk 9

Weights		Volume	
400 g	14 oz	1.75 litres	3 pints
425 g	15 oz	1.8 litres	3¼ pints
450 g	1 lb	2 litres	3½ pints
550 g	1¼ lb	2.1 litres	3¾ pints
675 g	1½ lb	2.25 litres	4 pints
900 g	2 lb	2.75 litres	5 pints
1.5 kg	3 lb	3.4 litres	6 pints
1.75 kg	4 lb	3.9 litres	7 pints
2.25 kg	5 lb	5 litres	8 pints (1 gal)

SOUPS and STARTERS

Andalusian gazpacho

This famous Spanish cold soup should be made in the summer when tomatoes are at their peak – sweet and full of flavour. It is quite the best thing you could want to eat on a hot day. Gazpacho is an easy dish – you do not need to peel the tomatoes and you can make it hours in advance. If the weather is very hot, add an ice cube to each bowl.

serves 4
preparation time: 30 minutes

2 slices of white bread, crusts removed

1 kg (2¹/₄ lb) ripe plum tomatoes

1 red pepper, seeds removed, cut into 4 pieces

3 garlic cloves, crushed

4 tablespoons sherry vinegar or wine vinegar, or to taste

5 tablespoons extra-virgin olive oil

1 teaspoon sugar, or to taste

salt and pepper

For the garnish:

¹/₂ cucumber, finely diced

¹/₂ red onion or 4 spring onions, finely chopped

¹/₂ green pepper, finely diced

2 Cut the tomatoes in half and remove the little hard bit at the stem end, then cut them again into quarters or eighths.

3 Blend the red pepper to a paste in a food processor. Add all the rest of the soup ingredients and blend to a light cream. Add a little cold water – about 100–150 ml (3¹/₂–5 fl oz) – to thin it, if necessary. Taste the soup and adjust the seasoning with more sugar, vinegar, salt or pepper.

1 Dry out the bread under the grill without browning it, turning the slices over once, then break it up into pieces.

4 Pour into a bowl, cover with cling film and chill for at least an hour in the refrigerator. Check the seasoning and serve in soup bowls, accompanied by the garnish ingredients, each on a separate little plate or in 3 piles on a large plate.

Chilled almond soup with garlic and grapes

This is another popular Andalusian soup, which is called *ajo blanco* (white garlic). There is meant to be a lot of garlic, and it is raw, but you can reduce the quantity if you prefer. Crush it in a garlic press or pound it to a paste with a little salt in a mortar. Choose good white bread from a country-style loaf and a mild-tasting extra-virgin olive oil. I always used to peel the grapes but recently I have stopped doing that and found the result just as good. You can make the soup several hours in advance.

serves 4
preparation time: 25 minutes

100 g (4 oz) day-old white bread, cut into slices, crusts removed

250 g (9 oz) blanched almonds

3 garlic cloves, crushed

500 ml (17 fl oz) iced water

120 ml (4 fl oz) extra-virgin olive oil, plus a little extra to serve

3 tablespoons sherry vinegar or white wine vinegar, or to taste

300 g (11 oz) white seedless grapes, or more, washed

salt

1 Put the bread in a small bowl, pour over just enough water to cover and leave to soak for a few minutes.

2 Grind the almonds very finely in a food processor. Squeeze the bread dry and add to the almonds with the garlic and a few tablespoons of the iced water. Process to a smooth paste.

3 With the food processor still running, add the olive oil in a slow stream. Then add the remaining cold water until the soup has a creamy consistency.

4 Pour into a serving bowl, season with salt and vinegar and stir in the grapes. Cover with cling film and chill for at least an hour. Serve drizzled with a little oil.

Spiced lentil soup

Lentil soup is an Egyptian favourite and part of my childhood memories. This homely version is simple and heart-warming.

serves 4
preparation time: 10 minutes
cooking time: 35–50 minutes

1 onion, chopped

1¹/₂ tablespoons olive oil

2 garlic cloves, crushed

³/₄ teaspoon ground cumin

³/₄ teaspoon ground coriander

150 g (5 oz) split red lentils

1.25 litres (2¹/₄ pints) chicken stock (you may use 1¹/₂–2 stock cubes)

juice of ¹/₂ lemon

salt and pepper

1 Fry the onion in the oil in a large saucepan until soft, stirring occasionally.

2 Stir in the garlic, cumin and coriander. When the aroma rises (in moments only), add the lentils and stock.

3 Bring to the boil and skim off any scum that appears on the surface. Reduce the heat and simmer for 30–45 minutes, until the lentils have disintegrated. Add salt if necessary (taking into account the saltiness of the stock cubes) and some pepper.

4 Thin with a little water if necessary. Stir in the lemon juice before serving.

Aubergine caviar

Often described as 'poor man's caviar', this is the commonest way of eating aubergines all around the Mediterranean. Use firm, medium-sized aubergines with a shiny black skin. The texture is better if you chop the flesh by hand rather than blending it in a food processor. If you want to prepare a large quantity for a party, instead of grilling the aubergines you can roast them in the hottest possible oven (lay them on a sheet of foil) for about 30 minutes, turning them on their side at least once.

serves 4
preparation time: 15 minutes
cooking time: about 15 minutes

2 aubergines, weighing
    approximately 675 g
    (1½ lb) in total
4 tablespoons extra-virgin
    olive oil
juice of ½ lemon, or more
    to taste
salt
chopped fresh parsley or
    black olives, to garnish
    (optional)

1 Prick the aubergines in a few places with a sharp knife to prevent them bursting. Place them under a hot grill and cook, turning occasionally, until they feel very soft and the skin is wrinkled.

2 Peel the aubergines, letting the flesh fall into a fine colander or a sieve. Chop the flesh with a sharp knife and mash to a purée with a fork or a wooden spoon, so that the juices escape through the holes of the colander or sieve.

3 Transfer the purée to a bowl and beat in the oil, lemon juice and some salt to taste. Garnish with chopped parsley or black olives before serving, if liked.

Carrot and potato appetizer

This homely Tunisian salad is easy to make and very tasty. Use old carrots and mealy potatoes. Serve it cold, with bread or toast for dipping.

serves 4
preparation time: 15 minutes

675 g (1¹/₂ lb) carrots, peeled

500 g (1 lb 2 oz) potatoes, peeled

2 garlic cloves, chopped

3–4 teaspoons ground cumin

5 tablespoons extra-virgin olive oil

2 tablespoons wine vinegar

a large pinch of chilli powder or cayenne pepper

salt

1 Slice the carrots and cut each potato into 2–4 pieces. Put them in a pan with some salt, the garlic and enough water to cover.

2 Bring to the boil, then reduce the heat and simmer until soft. Drain well and mash with a potato masher or a fork.

3 Put the carrot and potato purée in a serving bowl and stir in the remaining ingredients, adding more salt if necessary.

Bulgur and tomato salad

Kisir is a luscious and filling Turkish country salad. A touch of chilli gives it a thrilling zing. The bulgur does not need cooking, only soaking in water until it is tender.

serves 6–8
preparation time: 30 minutes, plus 20 minutes' standing

250 g (9 oz) bulgur (cracked wheat)

2 tablespoons tomato purée

5 tablespoons extra-virgin olive oil

juice of 1 lemon

1/3 teaspoon dried chilli flakes or a pinch of chilli powder, or to taste

1 fresh red or green chilli, very finely chopped

5 tablespoons chopped fresh flat-leaf parsley

3 sprigs of fresh mint, chopped

6 spring onions, finely chopped

2 large tomatoes, finely diced

salt

1 Put the bulgur in a bowl, pour plenty of boiling water over it and leave to stand for 20 minutes, or until the grain is just tender.

2 Drain the bulgur through a fine sieve or colander and squeeze the excess water out.

3 Add the tomato purée, oil, lemon juice, chilli flakes or powder and some salt and mix thoroughly. You can do this in advance.

4 Just before serving, mix in all
the remaining ingredients.

Couscous salad

This substantial salad is easy to make for a large company and can be prepared in advance, as it does not spoil. The couscous does not need cooking, only soaking in water until it is tender.

serves 6–8

preparation time: 30 minutes, plus about 50 minutes' standing

250 g (9 oz) couscous

300 ml (10 fl oz) cold water

juice of 1–1½ lemons, or to taste

6 tablespoons extra-virgin olive oil

grated zest of 1 lemon (optional)

3 firm, medium-sized tomatoes, diced

1 cucumber, peeled and diced

8 spring onions, sliced

4 tablespoons chopped fresh parsley

a few sprigs of fresh mint, chopped

12 black or green olives, pitted and chopped (optional)

salt and pepper

1 Put the couscous in a bowl, add the water and stir well. Leave to stand for about 20 minutes, until the water has been absorbed. Fluff it up by rubbing it between your hands and break up any lumps.

2 For the dressing, mix the lemon juice and olive oil with some salt and pepper and the lemon zest, if you like. Stir into the couscous and leave to stand for at least 30 minutes, so that it absorbs the dressing.

3 Just before serving, mix in all the remaining ingredients.

Greek country salad

This salad can be prepared in advance but it should be dressed only at the last minute. I like it kept simple, but possible additions are chopped fennel, wild marjoram, sprigs of mint, capers and sliced gherkins. Serve with good country bread.

serves 6
preparation time: 25 minutes

1 cos lettuce

2 large, ripe but firm tomatoes

1 cucumber

1 green pepper

1 large, mild red or white onion or 9 spring onions

250 g (9 oz) feta cheese, cut into small squares or broken into coarse pieces

12 or more black kalamata olives

For the dressing:

a good bunch of fresh flat-leaf parsley, coarsely chopped

6 tablespoons extra-virgin olive oil

juice of 1 lemon

salt and pepper

1 Shred the lettuce into wide ribbons with a sharp knife. Cut the tomatoes into wedges. Peel the cucumber, cut it lengthways in half, then slice it thickly.

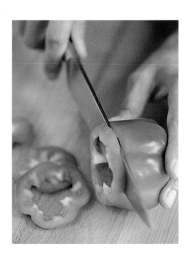

2 Remove the seeds from the green pepper and cut it into thin rings. If using 1 large onion, slice it thinly and separate the rings; if using spring onions, just slice them thinly.

3 Put the prepared vegetables into a large bowl with the feta cheese and olives.

4 Just before serving, mix all the ingredients for the dressing together. Pour the dressing over the salad and toss well.

Tunisian roasted salad

This salad is ubiquitous in Tunisia. The Tunisians call it *meshweya*, meaning 'roasted', because the vegetables are roasted or grilled – usually over a fire. It makes a very satisfying snack meal in itself.

serves 4–6
preparation time: 50 minutes
cooking time: 45 minutes–1 hour

3 onions

3 green or red peppers

3 tomatoes

200 g (7 oz) can of tuna in brine, drained and flaked

2 hard-boiled eggs, shelled and cut into wedges

1 tablespoon capers, rinsed and drained (optional)

8–12 green or black olives (optional)

50 g (2 oz) can of anchovies in oil, drained (optional)

4–5 tablespoons extra-virgin olive oil

juice of 1 lemon

1/2 teaspoon caraway seeds

salt and pepper

1 Pre-heat the oven to its hottest. Put the onions, peppers and tomatoes on a piece of foil on a baking sheet and place in the oven.

2 Remove the tomatoes as soon as the skins begin to loosen and they soften very slightly – this will take about 15 minutes. When they are cool enough to handle, skin them and cut into wedges.

3 Roast the peppers for another 15 minutes, or until the skins are browned and they feel soft, turning them once. Drop them into a plastic freezer bag and twist to close it; this loosens the skins further. When they are cool enough to handle, peel the peppers and remove the seeds, then cut each pepper into 8 ribbons from the stem end to the bottom.

5 Arrange the elements of the salad – onions, peppers, tomatoes, flaked tuna and eggs – on individual plates in a decorative way. A garnish of capers, olives and anchovies is optional. Mix the oil, lemon juice, salt, pepper and caraway seeds together and drizzle over the salad.

4 Take the onions out when they feel soft when you press them. They will take 15–30 minutes longer than the peppers. Leave until cool enough to handle, then peel them and cut into wedges.

Lentils and rice with caramelized onions

This is immensely popular in the eastern Mediterranean. It can be served warm or at room temperature, as a first course or as part of a light vegetarian meal, often accompanied by yoghurt. You can vary the proportions of lentils and rice. The generous quantity of dark, caramelized onions is the best part.

serves 6
preparation time: 15 minutes
cooking time: 1 hour 10 minutes

8 tablespoons extra-virgin olive oil (or more)

3 large onions, weighing approximately 675 g (1½ lb) in total, cut in half from the stem end and sliced

250 g (9 oz) large green or brown lentils

250 g (9 oz) long-grain rice

salt and pepper

1 Heat 3–4 tablespoons of the oil in a large pan, add the onions and cook, covered, over a very low heat, stirring occasionally, for about 20 minutes, until they soften. Continue cooking, uncovered, over a medium heat, stirring often, until the onions are golden.

2 Rinse the lentils in cold water and drain. Put them in a large saucepan, add 1 litre (1¾ pints) of water and bring to the boil. Reduce the heat and simmer for 20 minutes (do not add salt as this prevents them softening).

3 Add the rice and half the fried onions to the lentils, season with salt and pepper and stir well. Cook, covered, over a very low heat for another 20 minutes, or until the rice and lentils are tender, adding more water if the mixture becomes too dry.

4 Meanwhile, put the remaining onions back on the heat and fry over a medium to high heat, stirring frequently, until they are very dark brown – almost caramelized. Serve the lentils and rice warm or at room temperature in a wide, shallow dish, with the onions sprinkled on top and the remaining oil drizzled all over.

Roasted peppers and aubergines with yoghurt

Peppers and aubergines are the most popular vegetables around the Mediterranean and this is my favourite way of cooking them. I serve them hot as a side dish or cold as an appetizer. Yoghurt is a traditional Turkish accompaniment.

serves 4

preparation time: about 20 minutes

cooking time: about 15 minutes

2 medium-sized aubergines, weighing approximately 675 g (1½ lb) in total

2 fleshy red peppers

3 tablespoons extra-virgin olive oil

300 ml (10 fl oz) natural yoghurt or thick, Greek-style yoghurt

1 garlic clove, crushed (optional)

salt

1 Prick the aubergines in a few places with a sharp knife to prevent them exploding. Place the aubergines and peppers on a piece of foil on a baking sheet and place under a hot grill (or put the vegetables directly on a bar-becue grill over glowing embers).

2 Cook the peppers for about 10 minutes, turning them occasionally, until they soften and the skin is blackened and blistered. Put them in a plas-tic freezer bag (thinner plastic can melt with the heat), twist it closed and leave for 15–20 minutes (this helps to loosen the skins further; another way is to put them in a pan with a tight-fitting lid). When the peppers are cool enough to handle, peel them and remove the stems and seeds.

4 Cut the peppers and aubergines into wide strips, sprinkle lightly with salt and the olive oil and mix gently. If serving hot, heat through in the oven first. Accompany with the yoghurt, mixed, if you like, with the garlic.

3 Turn the aubergines too, as their skin wrinkles and darkens, until they feel soft when you press them with your finger; this should take about 15 minutes. Leave until cool enough to handle, then peel them straight into a colander. Press the flesh very gently, letting the juices drain out through the colander.

Pissaladière

This famous tart from Nice is like an onion pizza. It derives its name from the anchovy paste, *pissala*, which used to be brushed on it. I like to use the smaller quantity of onion given below but many Niçois prefer the larger amount.

serves 6
preparation time: 1 hour, plus
1¹/₄–2¹/₄ hours' rising
cooking time: about 1¹/₄ hours

For the dough:
15 g (¹/₂ oz) fresh yeast or
  1¹/₂ teaspoons dried yeast
¹/₂ teaspoon sugar
85 ml (3 fl oz) lukewarm water
250 g (9 oz) plain flour
1 egg, lightly beaten
³/₄ teaspoon salt
a few drops of olive oil

For the topping:
1–2 kg (2¹/₄–4¹/₂ lb) onions,
  thinly sliced
3–4 tablespoons extra-virgin
  olive oil
1 teaspoon each chopped
  fresh thyme and rosemary
12 or more anchovy fillets
  preserved in oil, cut in half
  lengthways
a few black olives, pitted
salt and pepper

1 Put the yeast and sugar in a bowl with the lukewarm water. Mix well and leave for about 10 minutes, until it froths.

2 Sift the flour into a large bowl and make a well in the centre. Put the egg and salt in the well and mix them into the flour.

3 Gradually add the yeast mixture. Begin by mixing it in with a fork, then work it in with your fingers, until the dough holds together in a ball. Add a little more flour if it is too sticky or a drop of water if it is too dry.

4 Turn the dough out onto a lightly floured work surface and knead vigorously for about 10 minutes, until it is smooth and elastic. Pour a drop or two of olive oil into the bowl and turn the ball of dough in it so that it becomes lightly oiled all over. This is to prevent a dry crust forming. Cover the bowl with cling film and leave to rise in a warm place for about 1–2 hours, until it doubles in bulk.

5 Meanwhile, make the filling. Cook the onions in the olive oil in a covered pan on a very low heat, stirring occasionally, for 30–40 minutes, until they are very soft but not coloured (it takes so long because of the large quantity). Add the herbs and some salt and pepper and cook for a few minutes longer.

6 Pre-heat the oven to 190°C/375°F/Gas Mark 5. Grease a pie plate or flan dish, about 25cm (10 in) in diameter, with oil. Punch the risen dough down, knead it lightly and then press it into the pie plate or flan dish with the palms of your hands.

7 Spread the onion mixture over the dough and make a lattice pattern of anchovy fillets on top. Put an olive in the middle of each square. Let the dough rise again for 10–15 minutes, then bake for 25–30 minutes, or until the bread base is cooked. Serve hot.

Cheese 'cigars'

These little Turkish pies make wonderful finger food. Filo pastry is available both fresh and frozen in packets that vary in weight (a common weight is 400 g/14 oz) and in the size and thinness of the sheets. A common size in supermarkets is 30 x 14 cm (12 x 5^1/$_2$ in), which is fine for this recipe.

makes 16
preparation time: 30 minutes
cooking time: 30 minutes

200 g (7 oz) feta cheese

1 egg, lightly beaten

a small bunch of fresh mint,
  parsley or dill, very finely
  chopped (optional)

16 sheets of filo pastry

3 tablespoons melted butter
  or oil

1 Pre-heat the oven to 180°C/350°F/Gas Mark 4. For the filling, mash the feta cheese with a fork and mix with the egg and the herbs, if using.

2 Take the sheets of filo out of the packet only when you are ready to use them, as they dry out easily. Keep them stacked up in a pile. Lightly brush half the top sheet lengthways with melted butter or oil and then fold it in half to make a long, narrow strip. Brush the top of the folded strip with butter or oil.

3 Take a heaped teaspoon of filling and place it at one end of the strip in a thin sausage shape along the short edge – about 2.5 cm (1 in) from it and from the 2 long edges.

4 Roll up with the filling inside, turning the long edges in about half way through rolling to enclose the filling. Repeat with the rest of the filo and filling.

5 Place the cigars close to each other on a greased baking tray and brush the tops with melted butter or oil. Bake in the preheated oven for 30 minutes, or until crisp and golden.

FISH and SHELLFISH

Seared tuna with tomato and lemon dressing

This appealing dressing is from Provence. You can use it with different kinds of fish, from cod to salmon, with fillets or steaks, whether grilled or pan-cooked. I like it at room temperature, but you may like to heat it through so that it is just warm.

Tuna is best eaten rare, simply seared, with the flesh still pink and almost raw inside.

serves 4
preparation time: 10 minutes
cooking time: 2 minutes

3 tablespoons olive oil

4 thick tuna steaks, weighing approximately 200 g (7 oz) each

salt

For the dressing:

6 tablespoons extra-virgin olive oil

4 tablespoons lemon juice

2 plum tomatoes, skinned and finely diced

salt and pepper

1 Prepare the dressing first. Whisk the oil with the lemon juice and some salt and pepper, then stir in the diced tomatoes.

2 Heat the olive oil in a large frying pan. Put in the tuna steaks and cook over a high heat for less than 1 minute on each side, sprinkling lightly with salt.

3 Cut into one piece of tuna with a sharp knife to check if it's done. The exact timing will depend on the thickness of the piece; it should be uncooked and pink inside. Serve the tuna steaks with the dressing poured on top.

Haddock with onion and honey fondue

You can make this Provençal dish with other kinds of white fish fillets. The onions must be meltingly soft, hence the name 'fondue', from the French *fondre*, meaning 'to melt'.

serves 4
preparation time: 15 minutes
cooking time: about 45 minutes

6 tablespoons extra-virgin
   olive oil
500 g (1 lb 2 oz) onions, cut
   in half and sliced
2 bay leaves
2 sprigs of fresh thyme
2 sprigs of fresh rosemary
2 tablespoons honey

2 teaspoons white wine
   vinegar
4 x 150 g (5 oz) pieces of
   haddock fillet, skinned
salt and plenty of pepper

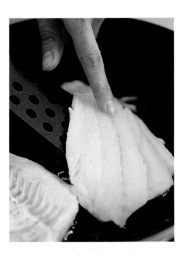

1 Heat 4 tablespoons of the oil in a wide pan, add the onions, bay leaves, thyme and rosemary and cook, covered, over a very low heat, for 20–30 minutes, stirring occasionally. The onions should be very soft and just beginning to colour (they will stew in their juices rather than fry).

2 Add the honey, wine vinegar and some salt and pepper and cook, uncovered, over a medium heat for another 10 minutes, until much of the liquid has evaporated and the onions are just very lightly golden.

3 Heat the remaining olive oil in a large frying pan. Put in the fish fillets and cook over a medium heat for 3–6 minutes, turning them over once and sprinkling both sides with salt; they are done when the flesh begins to flake if you cut into it with a sharp knife. Serve the haddock with the onions spread on top.

Red mullet in a saffron and ginger tomato sauce

Fish cooked in tomato sauce is ubiquitous in every Mediterranean country. This exquisitely flavoured sauce may also be used with other kinds of fish – small whole ones or fillets such as haddock, cod or salmon. If you find small red mullet, it is lovely to use them whole.

I extract the juice from fresh ginger by peeling it, cutting it into small pieces and crushing them in a garlic press, but you can just grate the ginger if you prefer.

> serves 2
> preparation time: 25 minutes
> cooking time: about 20 minutes

3 garlic cloves, chopped

1 fresh chilli, finely chopped

2–3 tablespoons extra-virgin olive oil

500 g (1 lb 2 oz) ripe tomatoes, skinned and chopped

1¹/₂ teaspoons sugar

¹/₄ teaspoon crushed saffron strands (see page 20) or saffron powder

4 cm (1¹/₂ in) piece of fresh root ginger, the juice squeezed out in a garlic press

2 medium-sized red mullet, cleaned and filleted

salt and pepper

1 In a frying pan, heat the garlic and chilli in the olive oil for moments only, stirring, until the aroma rises.

2 Add the tomatoes, sugar, saffron, ginger juice and some salt and pepper and simmer for 10 minutes.

3 Put the red mullet fillets in the tomato sauce and simmer for up to 6 minutes, turning the fish over once, until the flesh begins to flake when you cut into it with a sharp knife.

Cod with salsa verde

Salsa verde, a strongly flavoured Italian green sauce, makes a good accompaniment to cod. It also goes well with other white fish, such as haddock, halibut and monkfish, and with salmon and salmon trout. It is served at room temperature and keeps for days in the refrigerator. The fish can be grilled or poached in white wine but the simplest way to cook it is in a frying pan.

serves 4
preparation time: 15 minutes
cooking time: 4–10 minutes

3 tablespoons olive oil
4 x 150 g (5 oz) pieces of cod fillet, skinned
salt

For the salsa verde:
a very large bunch of fresh flat-leaf parsley, weighing about 50 g (2 oz), stalks removed
75 g (3 oz) pine nuts
5 small cocktail gherkins

8 green olives, pitted
2–3 garlic cloves, crushed
3 tablespoons wine vinegar or the juice of 1/2 lemon
about 120 ml (4 fl oz) mild extra-virgin olive oil
salt and pepper

1 Prepare the salsa verde first. Blend all the ingredients except the oil in a food processor. Then add the extra-virgin olive oil gradually – enough to give a creamy paste. Taste and adjust the seasoning if necessary.

2 Heat the olive oil in a large, preferably non-stick, frying pan that will hold the cod in one layer. Put in the fish and sprinkle with salt.

3 Cook over a low heat for 4–10 minutes (depending on the thickness of the fish), turning the fish over once and sprinkling it with salt. It is ready when the flesh is opaque and just begins to flake if you cut into it with a sharp knife. Serve accompanied by the sauce.

Marinated cod Moroccan-style

With its exotic flavours, this makes an exciting cold first course or buffet dish. The fish is quickly fried, then marinated in a beautifully aromatic dressing. Make it at least an hour before you need to serve it. You can use other firm-fleshed white fish, such as haddock or halibut.

serves 4
preparation time: 15 minutes
cooking time: 5–8 minutes, plus
    at least 1 hour's marinating

4–5 tablespoons plain flour
1/2–1 teaspoon ground cumin,
    or to taste
500 g (1 lb 2 oz) cod fillet,
    skinned and cut into 2.5 cm
    (1 in) pieces
olive oil for frying

For the marinade:
3–4 tablespoons extra-virgin
    olive oil
juice of 1/2 lemon
6 tablespoons chopped fresh
    coriander
1/2 mild onion, finely chopped
1/2 fresh chilli, seeded and
    finely chopped
1 garlic clove, crushed
salt

1 Mix the flour and cumin together. Roll the pieces of fish in this, turning to coat them lightly all over.

2 In a large frying pan, heat a layer of olive oil about 8 mm (1/3 in) deep. Add the cod and fry over a medium-high heat for 5–8 minutes, until golden, turning the pieces over once. Cut into a piece to check if it is done: the flesh should flake and have turned opaque. Drain on kitchen paper.

3 Mix all the marinade ingredients together in a bowl, add the fish and turn it over to coat. Leave in the refrigerator, covered with cling film, for at least an hour before serving.

Spicy prawns

This Moroccan way with prawns is quick to prepare and tastes wonderful. Use raw king prawns (they are grey and turn pink when cooked). Some supermarkets sell them ready peeled. You can also buy them frozen with their heads off from some fishmongers, in which case you may need double the weight.

serves 4
preparation time: 20 minutes
cooking time: about 3 minutes

600 g (1 lb 5 oz) raw king prawns, shell on, or 300 g (11 oz) peeled ones

4 tablespoons extra-virgin olive oil

4 garlic cloves, crushed

2 teaspoons paprika

1½ teaspoons ground cumin

3/4 teaspoon ground ginger

a good pinch of cayenne pepper or chilli powder

5 tablespoons chopped fresh coriander or parsley

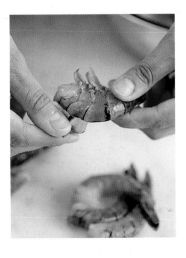

1 To peel the prawns, twist off their heads and pull off the 'legs'. Then break open the shell along the belly and peel it off (leave the tail on, if liked, for more attractive presentation). If you see a dark thread along the back, make a fine slit with a sharp knife and pull it out.

2 In a large frying pan, heat the oil with the garlic and spices, stirring, for seconds only, until the aroma rises.

3 Throw in the peeled prawns and fry quickly over a medium heat, stirring and turning them over, for about 1 minute, until they turn pink. Stir in the coriander or parsley towards the end.

Provençal prawns

Cognac and white wine give this sauce an exquisite flavour.
It is very good served with rice. Use raw king prawns, either
with the shells still on or ready peeled. If you buy frozen
prawns with their heads off, you may need double the weight.

serves 4
preparation time: 30 minutes
cooking time: 30 minutes

600 g (1 lb 5 oz) raw king
   prawns, shell on, or 300 g
   (11 oz) peeled ones

1 onion, chopped

2 tablespoons extra-virgin
   olive oil

2 garlic cloves, finely
   chopped

500 g (1 lb 2 oz) tomatoes,
   skinned and chopped

1 teaspoon sugar

1 fresh red chilli, finely
   chopped

3 tablespoons cognac

150 ml (5 fl oz) dry white wine

2 sprigs of fresh thyme

1 bay leaf

3 tablespoons chopped fresh
   flat-leaf parsley

salt

1 To peel the prawns, twist off
their heads and pull off the
'legs'. Then break open the
shell along the belly and peel
it off (leave the tail on, if
liked, for more attractive
presentation). If you see a
dark thread along the back,
make a fine slit with a sharp
knife and pull it out.

2 Fry the onion in the olive oil
in a large frying pan, stirring
occasionally, until it begins to
colour.

3 Add the garlic and, when the aroma rises, add all the remaining ingredients except the prawns and parsley. Simmer, uncovered, for about 20 minutes, until the sauce is reduced and aromatic.

4 Add the prawns and cook over a medium heat for 1–2 minutes, turning them over, until they turn pink. Serve hot, garnished with the parsley.

Mussels in white wine

This is the favourite way of eating mussels around
the western Mediterranean. Serve with good bread.

serves 4–6
preparation time: 35 minutes
cooking time: 15–20 minutes

2 kg (4¹/₂ lb) mussels

3 garlic cloves, finely
chopped

3 tablespoons extra-virgin
olive oil

600 ml (1 pint) dry white wine

4 tablespoons chopped fresh
flat-leaf parsley

1 Scrub the mussels, pull off
their beards and wash in
several changes of cold
water. If there are any open
mussels, check whether they
are still alive by tapping them
on a work surface or dipping
them in cold water – if they
do not close they should be
discarded. Also discard any
mussels that have broken
shells or that feel too heavy
or too light.

2 In a very large pan, heat the
garlic in the olive oil. As soon
as the aroma rises, add the
wine. Simmer for 10–15 minutes. The wine will reduce
and acquire a delicious, mel-
low flavour.

3 Add the mussels to the pan,
cover and leave over a very
high heat for 1–2 minutes,
until they open.

5 Strain the wine and mussel liquor through a fine sieve or one lined with muslin to catch any sand, then pour it over the mussels.

4 Using a slotted spoon, transfer the mussels to bowls or soup plates, discarding any that remain closed. Sprinkle with the parsley.

Italian fish soup

Every Italian seaport has its own special fish soup, or *zuppa di pesce*. This version can be put together quite quickly and the flavours are pure and delicate. Use a good, fruity dry white wine (I use Pinot Grigio) – it will make your soup a grand dish.

serves 4
preparation time: 30 minutes
cooking time: about 55 minutes

4–6 garlic cloves, chopped

1 small, fresh red chilli, seeded and chopped

2 tablespoons olive oil

8 plum tomatoes, skinned and roughly chopped

1 bottle of fruity, dry white wine

750 g (1¾ lb) small baking potatoes, peeled and cut into halves or quarters

2 teaspoons sugar, or to taste

500 g (1 lb 2 oz) haddock fillet, skinned and cut into 4 pieces

200 g (7 oz) peeled raw prawns

16–20 mussels, scrubbed and de-bearded (see page 72)

a bunch of fresh flat-leaf parsley, coarsely chopped

salt and pepper

1 Heat the garlic and chilli in the olive oil in a large, wide pan for moments only, until the garlic just begins to colour.

2 Add the tomatoes, white wine and potatoes and season with salt, pepper and the sugar. Add just enough water to cover the potatoes.

3 Bring to the boil and simmer with the lid on for about 40 minutes, until the potatoes are tender. Add the haddock and prawns and cook for 5 minutes longer.

4 Add the mussels and cook for a minute or so, until the shells open. Adjust the seasoning, if necessary, and serve sprinkled with the parsley.

POULTRY and MEAT

Chicken with rosemary

This Italian way of cooking chicken is so simple that you could easily adopt it for every day. Serve with boiled or mashed potatoes.

serves 4
preparation time: 10 minutes
cooking time: about 40 minutes

40g (1¹/₂ oz) butter

1 tablespoon extra-virgin olive oil

2–3 garlic cloves, cut in half

2 sprigs of fresh rosemary

1 chicken, weighing about 1.5 kg (3 lb), cut into quarters

175 ml (6 fl oz) dry white wine

salt and pepper

1 Heat the butter and oil in a large shallow frying pan with the garlic and rosemary.

2 When the mixture sizzles, put in the chicken and cook over a medium heat, turning the pieces, until they are coloured all over.

3 Sprinkle the chicken with salt and pepper, add the wine, then cover and simmer for 30 minutes, or until the chicken is very tender.

Poussins in a honey sauce with couscous stuffing

Like many festive dishes in Morocco, this is savoury and sweet. Some of the couscous stuffing goes inside the birds, the rest is to serve on the side. You could make it easier for yourself by serving it all on the side. A small poussin is not too much for one person but a large one should be cut in half to serve two.

Couscous is made from durum semolina. The traditional way of cooking it is by lengthy steaming. However, the commercial variety available in the UK has been pre-cooked and only needs water added and heating through.

serves 4

preparation time: 25 minutes, plus 15 minutes' standing time for the couscous

cooking time: 45–60 minutes

4 small poussins

40 g (1¹/2 oz) butter or 3 tablespoons sunflower oil

1¹/2 large onions, finely chopped or grated

2 garlic cloves, crushed

2 teaspoons ground cinnamon

¹/4 teaspoon ground ginger

¹/2 teaspoon crushed saffron strands or saffron powder (see page 20)

2 tablespoons honey

salt and plenty of pepper

For the couscous stuffing:

350 g (12 oz) couscous

¹/2–³/4 teaspoon salt

2–3 teaspoons caster sugar

2¹/2 tablespoons sunflower oil

1 teaspoon ground cinnamon

1¹/2 tablespoons orange-blossom water

50 g (2 oz) blanched almonds

50 g (2 oz) pistachio nuts

2 tablespoons raisins, soaked in warm water for 10 minutes and then drained

25 g (1 oz) butter

1 Prepare the stuffing first. Measure the volume of couscous in a measuring jug, then pour it into a bowl. Measure the same volume of warm water in the jug and mix in the salt. Add to the couscous and stir well so that the water is evenly absorbed. Leave to stand for about 15 minutes.

2 Stir in the sugar, 1½ tablespoons of the oil, the cinnamon and the orange-blossom
water and then rub the couscous between your hands to
break up any lumps.

3 Fry the almonds in the remaining sunflower oil, stirring, until
just lightly browned. Coarsely
chop them and mix them into
the couscous with the pistachios and the drained raisins.

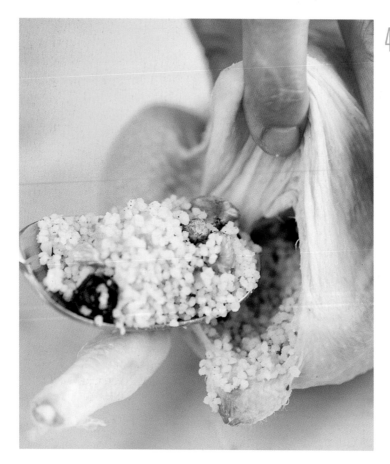

4 Fill each poussin with about
3 tablespoons of the stuffing.
They should not be too tight-
ly packed or the stuffing may
burst out. Use wooden tooth-
picks to close the openings,
securing the skin so that it
overlaps. Put the remaining
stuffing in a baking dish.

5 Put the butter or sunflower oil in a large, wide saucepan or pot and add the onions, garlic, cinnamon, ginger, saffron and some salt and pepper. Add about 300 ml (10 fl oz) water and then put in the poussins. Simmer gently, covered, for 30–45 minutes, until the birds are tender, adding more water if necessary and turning the birds over at least once, ending up with them breast-side down, so that they are well impregnated with the sauce.

6 If necessary, lift out one poussin to make a little room in the pan and stir in the honey. Then return the poussin to the pan and continue to cook for about 15 minutes, until the flesh is meltingly tender.

7 Pre-heat the oven to 200°C/400°F/Gas Mark 6. About 25 minutes before you are ready to serve, heat the stuffing through, covered with foil, in the oven, then stir in the butter. Serve the poussins accompanied by the extra stuffing.

Chicken with pickled lemons and olives

I love the taste of lemons pickled (or preserved) in salt. They lose their sharpness and acquire a special flavour. At every vegetable market in North Africa, and now also in the south of France, there are stalls laden with huge piles of soft lemons, oozing with juice, next to several varieties of olives. The two are often used together. You can now find pickled lemons and Moroccan olives in supermarkets. In this recipe the lemon is added towards the end of cooking but some cooks like to use a little chopped lemon to flavour the sauce during the cooking.

serves 4
preparation time: 20 minutes
cooking time: about 45 minutes

1 large chicken, cut into quarters

3 tablespoons vegetable oil or extra-virgin olive oil

1 large onion, grated or very finely chopped

2–3 garlic cloves, crushed

1/4 teaspoon crushed saffron strands (see page 20) or saffron powder

1/2 – 3/4 teaspoon ground ginger

11/2 teaspoons ground cinnamon

11/2 large or 3 small pickled lemons, rinsed and cut into quarters or thin strips

12–16 green or violet olives, soaked in 2 changes of water for 30 minutes and then drained

salt and pepper

1 Put the chicken pieces in a large, wide saucepan with all the ingredients except the preserved lemons and the olives. Half cover with water and bring just to the boil.

2 Reduce the heat, then cover the pan and simmer for about 45 minutes, until the chicken is so tender that the flesh can be pulled off the bone easily and the liquid is reduced to a thick sauce. Turn the chicken pieces over a few times during cooking and add a little more water if necessary.

3 Stir the lemon peel and olives into the sauce for the last 15 minutes of cooking. Some people like to add the lemon right at the very end.

Chicken with tomatoes and honey

This Moroccan *tagine* is one of my favourites. The chicken cooks in the juice from the tomatoes, which reduces to a sumptuous, thick, honeyed – almost caramelized – sauce. And it looks beautiful, too. Don't be worried about the large quantity of tomatoes; they will reduce right down.

One of the peculiarities of the Moroccan style of cooking – and of Fez in particular – is that they put all the ingredients in the pot at the same time, rather than frying the basic flavourings in the oil first.

serves 4
preparation time: 30 minutes
cooking time: about 1¼ hours

1 large chicken, cut into quarters

3 tablespoons sunflower oil or vegetable oil

1 large onion, grated or finely chopped

1 kg (2¼ lb) tomatoes, skinned and chopped

½ teaspoon ground ginger

1 teaspoon ground cinnamon

½ teaspoon crushed saffron strands (see page 20) or saffron powder

2 tablespoons clear (liquid) honey, or to taste (Moroccans use up to 4 tablespoons)

50 g (2 oz) blanched almonds, coarsely chopped

1 tablespoon sesame seeds

salt and pepper

1 Put all the ingredients except the honey, almonds, sesame seeds and 1 tablespoon of the oil in a large pan. Cover and cook over a low heat, turning the chicken pieces over occasionally, for about 1 hour, until the flesh is so tender that it can be pulled off the bone easily.

2 Remove the chicken pieces from the pan and keep warm. Cook the sauce over a medium heat until it has reduced to a thick, sizzling cream. Stir as it begins to caramelize and be careful that it does not stick or burn. Stir in the honey. Return the chicken pieces to the sauce and heat through.

3 Heat the chopped almonds in the remaining oil in a frying pan for moments only, then add the sesame seeds and stir them over a low heat for a few moments, until lightly coloured. Serve the chicken hot, covered with the sauce and sprinkled with the almonds and sesame seeds.

Sautéed pork medallions with Marsala

This Sicilian dish could not be easier. Use a sweet Marsala wine rather than a dry one. Serve with mashed or boiled potatoes.

serves 4
preparation time: 5 minutes
cooking time: about 10 minutes

2 pork fillets, weighing
    approximately 1 kg (2¼ lb)
    in total
4 tablespoons sunflower oil
150 ml (5 fl oz) Marsala
salt and pepper

1 Cut the pork fillets into medallion slices about 1 cm (½ in) thick.

2 Heat the sunflower oil in a large frying pan, add the pieces of meat and sauté quickly over a high heat until browned on both sides.

3 Sprinkle with salt and pepper and pour in the Marsala. Cook for a few minutes, until the meat is cooked through and the liquid has reduced a little. Serve immediately.

Greek stifatho

This heart-warming winter stew takes a long time to cook but does not need to be watched. It is peeling a large number of baby onions that is time-consuming. You will need a very large pan or casserole to cook the stew in. Serve with crusty bread, rice or potatoes.

serves 6–8
preparation time: 25 minutes
cooking time: about 2 hours

1 kg (2¼ lb) small pickling onions

1 kg (2¼ lb) stewing beef (or brisket) or pork, cut into 4 cm (1½ in) cubes

1 bottle of red wine

6 peppercorns

5 cloves

½–1 teaspoon ground allspice

4 tablespoons red or white wine vinegar

4 tablespoons extra-virgin olive oil

salt

1 Poach the pickling onions in a large pan of boiling water for 2–3 minutes to loosen their skins and make peeling easier. Then drain and peel them.

2 Put all the ingredients in a large pan or casserole and barely cover with water. Bring to the boil and skim off any scum that gathers on the surface.

3 Cover the pan and simmer over a very low heat for about 2 hours, or until the meat is very tender, adding more water if necessary to keep the meat just covered. Taste and adjust the seasoning, then serve.

Lamb tagine with prunes

The name *tagine* is derived from the clay dish with a cone-shaped lid in which stews such as this one are traditionally cooked. This is one of the most popular fruit *tagines* of North Africa. It is eaten with bread there, but restaurants in Paris, where it is also popular, serve it with plain couscous. It is usually made quite sweet with sugar or honey, but you may prefer to omit these.

serves 6
preparation time: 15 minutes
cooking time: about 2 1/4 hours

1 kg (2 1/4 lb) boned shoulder of lamb, cut into 6 or 12 pieces (trim off only some of the fat)

4 tablespoons sunflower oil or vegetable oil

3/4 teaspoon ground ginger

1/4 teaspoon crushed saffron strands (see page 20) or saffron powder

2 teaspoons ground cinnamon

1/3 teaspoon ground black pepper

1 large onion, finely chopped or grated

250 g (9 oz) Californian pitted prunes

2 tablespoons sugar or clear (liquid) honey (optional)

100 g (4 oz) sesame seeds or blanched almonds, coarsely chopped

salt

1 Put the meat in a large, wide pan with 3 tablespoons of the oil, plus the ginger, saffron, cinnamon, black pepper, onion and some salt. Add just enough water to cover and stir well.

2 Bring just to the boil, then reduce the heat and simmer gently, covered, for 1 1/2 hours, until the meat is very tender. Add a little more water during cooking, if necessary, to keep the meat just covered.

3 Add the prunes and cook, uncovered, for 30 minutes, until the liquid has reduced to a thick sauce. Stir in the sugar or honey, if using, and cook for 10 minutes more.

4 Toast the sesame seeds or chopped almonds for moments only in the remaining oil in a frying pan, stirring until just lightly coloured. Serve the *tagine* in a wide, shallow dish with the sesame seeds or almonds sprinkled on top.

Tagine of meatballs in tomato sauce with eggs

This tastes so good and also looks beautiful. You will need a large frying pan or a paella pan that can go to the table. In Morocco the cooking is finished in a wide, earthenware *tagine*, which goes on top of the fire. Serve with plenty of warm bread.

serves 6
preparation time: 45 minutes
cooking time: about 50 minutes

675 g (1½ lb) minced lamb or beef

1 onion, very finely chopped or grated

3 tablespoons finely chopped fresh flat-leaf parsley

a pinch of chilli powder, or to taste

1 teaspoon ground cinnamon

½ teaspoon ground ginger

1 teaspoon ground cumin

vegetable oil for shallow-frying

6 eggs

salt and pepper

For the tomato sauce:

2 onions, chopped

2 tablespoons olive oil

2 garlic cloves, crushed

675 g (1½ lb) tomatoes, skinned and chopped

1–2 teaspoons sugar, to taste

1 small, fresh chilli, seeded and chopped (optional)

3 tablespoons chopped fresh flat-leaf parsley

3 tablespoons chopped fresh coriander

salt

1 First make the sauce, using a large, shallow pan that you can bring to the table. Fry the onions in the oil until soft, then stir in the garlic. Add the tomatoes, sugar, the chilli, if using, and some salt. Mix well and simmer for 20 minutes, until the sauce has reduced and thickened.

2 Meanwhile, make the meatballs. Mix together the minced meat, onion, parsley, spices and some salt and pepper and gently knead to a soft paste with your hands.

3 Rub your hands with a little oil so that the meat does not stick, then roll the mixture into marble-sized balls and place them side by side on a plate.

4 Heat a thin layer of vegetable oil in a large frying pan and fry the meatballs briefly in it in batches, shaking the pan and turning the meatballs to brown them all over. They should still be pink inside. Lift out with a slotted spoon and leave to drain on kitchen paper.

5 Add the parsley and coriander to the sauce, put in the meatballs and simmer for about 5 minutes, until they are cooked through.

6 Break the eggs over the sauce and cook until the whites have set. Serve immediately.

PASTA, GRAINS and VEGETABLES

Spaghetti with garlic, herbs and olive oil

Spaghetti alle erbe is a Sicilian dish. I like using masses of herbs – at least 4 tablespoons per person – and plenty of garlic. You can chop the herbs by hand or in a food processor. If the taste of raw garlic is too strong for you, you could fry it in 1 tablespoon of oil for seconds only, until the sweet aroma rises.

This dish is not served with grated cheese. The best spaghetti to buy is the one made with durum wheat semolina.

serves 4
preparation time: 15 minutes
cooking time: 10–12 minutes

4 garlic cloves or more, crushed

a large bunch of fresh flat-leaf parsley, finely chopped

a large bunch of fresh basil, finely chopped

a large bunch of fresh mint, finely chopped

1/2 small, fresh red chilli, very finely chopped or pounded (optional)

120–150 ml (4–5 fl oz) extra-virgin olive oil

400 g (14 oz) spaghetti

salt

1 Prepare the sauce first. Mix the garlic, herbs and chilli, if using, with the olive oil in a large serving bowl. Add a little salt and mix well.

2 Put the spaghetti in a large pan of boiling salted water, gently pushing it in. Keep the water at a gentle rolling boil and cook for 10–12 minutes, until the spaghetti is *al dente* – tender but still firm to the bite. Drain quickly, keeping about half a cupful of the cooking water.

3 Toss the spaghetti with the oil and herb mixture, adding a little of the reserved cooking water if necessary, so that the spaghetti slides smoothly. Serve immediately.

Pasta with tomato sauce, courgettes and aubergines

I discovered this way of serving pasta, with fried courgettes and aubergines on a separate plate, in Sicily.

serves 4
preparation time: 30 minutes,
  plus 30 minutes–1 hour draining
cooking time: about 1 hour

2 medium aubergines, cut lengthways in half and thinly sliced into half-moon shapes

6 courgettes, thinly sliced

olive oil for deep-frying

400 g (14 oz) spaghetti

salt and pepper

freshly grated pecorino *sardo* or Parmesan cheese, to serve

For the tomato sauce:

1 onion, chopped

2 tablespoons olive oil

2 garlic cloves, finely chopped

1/2 small, fresh chilli, finely chopped (optional)

750 g (1 3/4 lb) tomatoes, skinned and chopped

1 teaspoon sugar

a good bunch of fresh basil, coarsely chopped

salt and pepper

1 Sprinkle the aubergines and courgettes with salt and leave them to drain in a colander for 30 minutes–1 hour.

2 For the tomato sauce, fry the onion in the olive oil until soft, then add the garlic and chilli, if using, and stir for a moment or two.

3 Add the tomatoes, sugar and some salt and pepper and cook for about 25 minutes, until the sauce has reduced to a thick consistency. Stir in the basil towards the end.

4 Rinse the aubergines and courgettes and dry them on kitchen paper. Deep-fry quickly in hot olive oil until lightly browned on both sides, then drain on kitchen paper. Arrange in a heatproof dish to heat through under the grill when the pasta is ready.

5 Push the pasta gradually into a large pan of boiling salted water. Keep the water at a gentle rolling boil and cook for 10–12 minutes, until the pasta is *al dente* – tender but still firm to the bite. Drain quickly and toss with the tomato sauce. Briefly heat the vegetable slices under a hot grill and then present them on a separate serving dish. Serve with freshly grated pecorino *sardo* or Parmesan cheese.

Spiced saffron rice

Yellow rice is a celebratory festive dish in the Middle East. This spiced version is exquisite and very aromatic. You can make it in advance and heat it through in the oven, covered with foil, before serving.

serves 6
preparation time: 15 minutes
cooking time: 30 minutes

500 g (1 lb 2 oz) basmati rice

900 ml (1½ pints) chicken stock (made using 1½ stock cubes)

1 teaspoon cardamom seeds (Indian stores sell them out of the pod)

6 cloves

3 cinnamon sticks, about 7.5 cm (3 in) long

½ teaspoon crushed saffron strands (see page 20) or saffron powder

65 g (2½ oz) butter, cut into small pieces, or 5 tablespoons sunflower oil

3 tablespoons pine nuts

3 tablespoons coarsely chopped almonds

3 tablespoons coarsely chopped pistachio nuts

salt and pepper

1 To wash the rice, put it in a bowl and pour hot water over it, then rinse under cold running water in a fine colander or sieve.

2 In a large pan, bring the stock to the boil with the cardamom seeds, cloves and cinnamon sticks and simmer for 10 minutes. Add the saffron and some salt and pepper and then add the rice.

3 Let it come to the boil again and stir well, then lower the heat to a minimum, cover the pan and cook for about 20 minutes, until little holes appear on the surface and the rice is tender. Gently stir in the butter or oil and add more salt to taste, if necessary.

4 Toast the pine nuts and almonds very briefly in a small, lightly oiled pan, shaking the pan, until they just begin to colour. Serve the rice hot, in a mound, sprinkled with the pine nuts, almonds and pistachios.

5 Alternatively, spread the nuts over the bottom of a ring mould, press the rice firmly down on top of them and turn out.

Bulgur pilaf

Bulgur (cracked wheat) makes satisfying comfort food. It is quick and easy to prepare and can be served as a side dish. It is something I am sure you will want to adopt. Use either the coarse-ground bulgur, found in Middle Eastern shops, or the medium-ground one that is now commonly available in super-markets. About one and a half times the volume of water or stock is needed. You can measure it by the cup if you want to make only a small quantity. Adding the optional currants or raisins and pine nuts gives a richer version, but the simple, plain one is also delicious.

serves 6–8
preparation time: 10 minutes,
  plus 10 minutes' standing time
cooking time: 10–15 minutes

1 litre (1³/₄ pints) water or
  chicken stock (you may use
  2 stock cubes)
500 g (1 lb 2 oz) coarse- or
  medium-ground bulgur
65 g (2¹/₂ oz) butter, cut into
  small pieces, or 5 tablespoons vegetable oil
50 g (2 oz) currants or raisins,
  soaked in water and
  drained (optional)
100 g (4 oz) pine nuts,
  toasted (optional)
salt and pepper

1 Bring the water or stock to the boil in a large pan and add the bulgur.

2 Add some salt and pepper, stir well and cook, covered, over a low heat for 10–15 minutes, until the grain is almost tender and all the liquid has been absorbed, adding a little more water if it becomes too dry.

3 Stir in the butter or oil, then
remove the pan from the heat
and leave to stand, covered,
for about 10 minutes to allow
the wheat to swell and
become tender before serving.
If using the currants or raisins
and pine nuts, fold them in
gently at the same time as
the butter or oil.

Baked tomatoes à la provençale

This is a simple and lovely way of preparing tomatoes, to be eaten hot or warm. It is also a Neapolitan speciality. To make your own breadcrumbs, dry out 2–3 slices of white bread, crusts removed, under the grill, without letting them colour, and then put them through a food processor.

serves 4–8
preparation time: 25 minutes
cooking time: 20–30 minutes

4 large, ripe but firm tomatoes

1 teaspoon sugar

40 g (1½ oz) fresh bread-
  crumbs

4 garlic cloves, crushed

4 tablespoons finely chopped
  fresh parsley or marjoram

6 tablespoons extra-virgin
  olive oil

salt and pepper

1 Pre-heat the oven to 190°C/375°F/Gas Mark 5. Cut the tomatoes in half and put them cut-side up in a greased, shallow baking dish. Sprinkle each with a pinch of the sugar and then lightly with salt.

2 Mix the rest of the ingredients together, adding a little salt.

3 Spread the breadcrumb mixture on top of the tomato halves. Bake for 20–30 minutes, until the tomatoes are soft but still hold their shape. Check them occasionally to make sure they don't fall apart.

Aubergines Parmigiana

In this famous Italian dish, aubergine slices are baked with tomatoes and cheese. Grilling the aubergines instead of frying them – which makes them soak up too much oil – results in a lighter version, which I prefer.

serves 4
preparation time: 40 minutes
cooking time: about 1 hour
  10 minutes

3 medium aubergines,
  weighing approximately
  675 g (1¹/₂ lb) in total, cut
  crossways into slices 1 cm
  (¹/₂ in) thick

a bland extra-virgin olive
  oil or sunflower oil, for
  brushing

1–2 balls of mozzarella
  cheese, diced

4 tablespoons freshly grated
  Parmesan cheese

salt

For the tomato sauce:

1 garlic clove, crushed or
  finely chopped

2 tablespoons olive oil

550 g (1¹/₄ lb) ripe plum
  tomatoes, skinned and
  finely chopped

1 teaspoon sugar

a few sprigs of fresh basil or
  mint, coarsely chopped

salt and pepper

1 Pre-heat the oven to 180°C/350°F/Gas Mark 4. To make the tomato sauce, fry the garlic in the oil for seconds only, until the aroma rises. Add the tomatoes, sugar and a little salt and pepper. Cook, uncovered, for 15–20 minutes, until the sauce has reduced and thickened, then stir in the herbs.

2 Arrange the aubergine slices on a large piece of foil on a baking sheet. Brush them with oil and sprinkle lightly with salt.

4 Arrange the aubergine slices in a 25 cm (10 in) ovenproof dish, cover with the tomato sauce and sprinkle the mozzarella and Parmesan on top. Bake for about 40 minutes, until lightly browned. Serve hot.

3 Cook the aubergines under a hot grill, turning once, until lightly browned (they can be left a little underdone and their skin tough as they will cook further and become soft in the oven).

Potato cake

This Tunisian speciality is easy to make and delicious.
It can be eaten hot or cold and is ideal to take on a picnic.

serves 4
preparation time: 20 minutes
cooking time: about 45 minutes

450 g (1 lb) floury potatoes,
   peeled and cut into chunks

1 large onion, chopped

3 tablespoons vegetable oil
   or olive oil

3 eggs, lightly beaten

4 tablespoons chopped fresh
   flat-leaf parsley

salt and pepper

1 Cook the potatoes in boiling salted water until tender, then drain and mash them.

2 Fry the onion in 2 tablespoons of the oil until soft and golden, stirring occasionally.

3 Beat the eggs into the potatoes with a fork. Then stir in the fried onion and parsley and season with salt and pepper.

4 Heat the remaining oil in a small, non-stick frying pan and pour in the potato mixture. Cook over a low heat until it is set underneath. Then place under a hot grill until the top is firm and lightly coloured. Turn out and serve hot or cold.

Spinach tian

A *tian* is the clay dish used for baking in the South of France. People always complain that they can't get vegetables in French restaurants but you can in the south. This creamy combination of spinach and rice makes a wholesome vegetarian main dish. Buy young spinach leaves. They are often sold ready-washed in packs in supermarkets.

serves 4–6
preparation time: 20 minutes
cooking time: about 40 minutes

550 g (1¼ lb) young spinach
120 g (4½ oz) long grain rice
4 eggs
300 ml (10 fl oz) milk
a pinch of nutmeg
salt and pepper

1 Pre-heat the oven to 190°C/ 375°F/Gas Mark 5. Wash the spinach if necessary. Bring about 1 litre (1¾ pints) of lightly salted water to the boil in a large pan – you will need a very large pan because spinach is so bulky. Add the rice to the pan and cook, covered, over a low heat for about 10 minutes.

2 Press the spinach on top, put the lid on and, as soon as the leaves wilt and crumple into a soft mass (this takes a minute or so), drain the rice and spinach through a colander with small holes. Set aside.

3 Beat the eggs together in a large bowl and gradually mix in the milk.

4 Add the spinach and rice, season with salt, pepper and nutmeg and mix very well. Pour into a lightly greased shallow baking dish and bake for 30 minutes, or until set.

Fried eggs with peppers and tomatoes

Served with bread, this makes a good quick snack. You could add capers and olives, but I like it best as it is.

serves 4
preparation time: 15 minutes
cooking time: 15–20 minutes

2 red or green peppers,
   seeded and cut into ribbons
3 tablespoons vegetable oil or
   extra-virgin olive oil
4 garlic cloves, sliced
4 tomatoes, skinned and cut
   into quarters
4 eggs
salt and pepper

1 In a large frying pan, over a medium heat, fry the peppers in the oil, stirring and turning over the pieces until they soften.

2 Add the garlic and, when it just begins to colour, add the tomatoes and some salt and pepper. Cook until the tomatoes soften.

3 Break the eggs in whole, season lightly again with salt and cook until the eggs set. Serve immediately.

Stuffed mushrooms

This is a Provençal and Ligurian way of preparing mushrooms. It makes an ideal first course or side dish. The French put in cognac, Italians often use rum.

serves 3–6
preparation time: 10 minutes
cooking time: 25 minutes

6 large, flat Portabello mushrooms

extra-virgin olive oil

2 good slices of white bread,
crusts removed

5 tablespoons finely chopped
fresh parsley

2–3 garlic cloves, crushed

3 tablespoons cognac

salt and pepper

1 Pre-heat the oven to 200°C/400°F/Gas Mark 6. Wipe the mushrooms with a damp cloth, if necessary. Cut off the stalks and set aside.

2 Heat a thin layer of olive oil in a large frying pan and sauté the mushrooms briefly over a medium heat for about 5 minutes, sprinkling lightly with salt and pepper and turning them over once. Arrange them, stem side up, in a flat, heatproof dish.

3 To make the stuffing, chop the mushroom stalks and crumble the bread finely. You can do this in a food processor, if you like, with the parsley.

4 Place the mushroom stalks, bread and parsley in a bowl and add as much garlic as you like, plus a little salt and pepper. Moisten with the cognac and 3–4 tablespoons of olive oil and mix well.

5 Press a little stuffing over each mushroom and bake for about 20 minutes, or until the mushrooms are tender.

Menus

In the Mediterranean, mealtimes are taken seriously. To enter into the spirit of Mediterranean eating you must enjoy food right from the planning, shopping and cooking stages to sitting down finally at the table. When you sit down to eat, do so in a happy and relaxed mood. It should be a convivial occasion – a ceremony and a celebration. Mediterraneans have a reputation for easy-going *joie de vivre*, particularly at the dinner table, so relax and take time to enjoy the food you have prepared in the company of your guests.

When planning a meal, you can choose an all-Moroccan, or all-Turkish, all-French or Italian menu, but you can also put together dishes from different countries as they mix and go very well together, being part of the same Mediterranean culture. I have given menu suggestions but you must please yourself and experiment a little. Choose a variety of colours – red peppers, tomatoes and black olives are always pleasing to the eye – and different flavours and textures in your first and second courses. A meal can be made up of several appetizers or of one main dish, such as a complex salad or a rich soup served with bread. Always provide good bread and wine as these are the staples of Mediterranean eating. Do not worry about matching wines with specific foods, as generally they all go well – we are long past the days when we thought fish always had to be partnered with white wine! And do not feel you have to buy an expensive wine – experiment and find a few that you enjoy. In the Muslim Mediterranean they serve fruit juices or a yoghurt drink. Their fresh, cool flavours often provide a good alternative to wine, particularly in hot weather.

Mediterranean desserts include ice creams, sorbets, milky puddings, fruity desserts, and syrupy, nutty pastries. I have not included recipes for desserts in this book as they are not a common feature of everyday eating in the Mediterranean. But the usual way to end a meal is with fruit. The most common are figs, grapes, apricots, dates, melons and watermelons, peaches, plums, cherries, apples, pears and oranges. A good way of serving fruit at a dinner party is to wash or peel and cut up a selection and arrange it attractively on a platter. Another Mediterranean tradition is to offer dried fruit and nuts with coffee.

Mediterranean Feast for 6

Roasted Peppers and Aubergines with
Yoghurt

Red Mullet in a Saffron and Ginger
Tomato Sauce

Bulgur Pilaf

Middle Eastern Medley for 4

Tunisian Roasted Salad

Chicken with Pickled Lemons and Olives

Spiced Saffron Rice

Moroccan Dinner Party for 6

Spicy Prawns

Lamb Tagine with Prunes, served with
plain couscous

Romantic Meal for 2

Chilled Almond Soup with Garlic
and Grapes

Poussins in a Honey Sauce with
Couscous Stuffing

Family Supper for 4

Carrot and Potato Appetizer

Tagine of Meatballs in Tomato Sauce
with Eggs

Vegetarian Supper for 4

Andalusian Gazpacho

Aubergines Parmigiana

Bulgur and Tomato Salad

Greek Supper for 4

Greek Country Salad

Greek Stifatho with crusty bread

Summer Buffet Party for 12

Aubergine Caviar
with crudités

Cheese 'Cigars'

Stuffed Mushrooms

Marinated Cod
Moroccan-style

Pissaladière

Couscous Salad

Potato Cake

Al Fresco Sunday Lunch for 8

Roasted Peppers and Aubergines
with Yoghurt

Lentils and Rice with
Caramelized Onions

Seared Tuna with Tomato and
Lemon Dressing

Spinach Tian

Index